MW01601345

30-Day Poetry Devotional:

Words of Strength and Light

Dedication:

To every soul searching for light in the shadows, May these words remind you—you are seen, you are strong, and you are never alone.

Table of Contents:

Foreword:

In a world full of noise and uncertainty,

may these poems serve as whispers of

courage, affirmations of hope, and

reminders of your divine purpose. Let each

day be a sacred pause to reconnect with

the light within you.

Day 1: Rise Again

When darkness falls, and hope feels thin,

Remember, child, you're built to win.

Storms may rage, and winds may blow,

But in your heart, the fire will glow.

So rise again, though weak you feel,

For faith and love can always heal.

Your story isn't over yet—

Stand tall, believe, and don't forget.

"Though the righteous fall seven times, they rise again." — Proverbs 24:16

Day 2: The Power Within

A mountain stands before your way,

Too high to climb, too fierce to stay.

But deep inside, there burns a spark,

A guiding light within the dark.

The strength you need is in your soul,

It fuels your fight, it makes you whole.

No wall too strong, no tide too high—

The power within will lift you high.

"I can do all things through Christ who strengthens me." — Philippians 4:13

Day 3: Unshaken

The earth may quake beneath your feet,

The sky may roar with storms that meet.

But planted firm, you will not break,

Your faith, your peace, none can take.

Through trials fierce and winds so wild,

God holds you still, His precious child.

Unshaken now, unshaken then,

Stand strong in Him, again, and again.

"Truly he is my rock and my salvation; he is my fortress, I will never be shaken." — Psalm 62:2

Day 4: The Waiting Season

The seed is sown, but nothing grows,

The waiting time, oh, how it slows.

Yet deep beneath the quiet ground,

Life is forming, strong and sound.

Do not despair, though time feels long,

Your harvest comes, stay brave, stay strong.

For what you've planted, faith has seen—

Soon will bloom what once was just a dream.

"Let us not become weary in doing good, for at the proper time we will reap a harvest if we do not give up."
— Galatians 6:9

Day 5: Light in the Valley

The valley deep, the shadows tall,

You walk alone, you feel so small.

But light is near, just up ahead,

A hand unseen, a path well-spread.

For even here, where dark seems king,

The dawn will rise, the birds will sing.

You are not lost, nor left behind—

God's light still shines, though hard to find.

"Even though I walk through the darkest valley, I will fear no evil, for you are with me." — Psalm 23:4

Day 6: Courage to Begin

A thousand steps seem much too far,

A dream can feel like chasing stars.

But every journey, every flight,

Begins with faith, begins tonight.

So take the step, embrace the call,

You were not made to fear or fall.

With every move, with every try,

Your wings will spread, your soul will fly.

"Be strong and courageous. Do not be afraid; do not be discouraged, for the Lord your God will be with you wherever you go." — Joshua 1:9

Day 7: A New Thing

Behold, a new thing now is near,

Let go of yesterday's old fear.

The past has passed, its hold is weak,

Step forward now, embrace and seek.

A road untraveled, fresh and bright,

A dawn of mercy, filled with light.

The old is gone, the chains unbound,

The grace of God now fills the ground.

"See, I am doing a new thing! Now it springs up; do you not perceive it?"

— Isaiah 43:19

Day 8: When You Feel Weary

Come lay it down, the weight, the care,

For heaven's hands are strong to bear.

Your weary soul, your heavy heart,

He lifts, He holds, He sets apart.

You were not meant to walk alone,

Nor fight each battle on your own.

Rest, dear soul, breathe in His peace,

Let all your striving now release.

"Come to me, all you who are weary and burdened, and I will give you rest."

— Matthew 11:28

Day 9: The Masterpiece

You are no accident, no stray,

No work unfinished, no cast away.

Each stroke, each line, each mark divine,

The Artist's hand shapes every sign.

A masterpiece, though still in mold,

A story great, a life untold.

So trust the work, embrace the plan,

You are His art—His heart,

Made by His hand.

"For we are God's masterpiece.

He has created us anew in Christ

Jesus." — Ephesians 2:10

Day 10: Just Keep Walking

The road is long, the way unsure,

But take one step, your faith is secure.

For mountains move when feet press on,

And battles yield when hope is strong.

So do not stop, though fears arise,

Your strength is drawn from endless skies.

The path ahead may twist and bend,

But walk in faith—you'll reach the end.

"For we walk by faith, not by sight."

— 2 Corinthians 5:7

Day 11: Faith Over Fear

Fear will whisper, loud and cruel,

That you are weak, that you're the fool.

But faith will roar and stand up tall,

Declaring you will never fall.

Choose faith, not sight,

when paths aren't clear,

Walk boldly on, dismiss the fear.

For God walks with you, step by step,

And every promise, He has kept.

"Do not fear, for I am with you."

— Isaiah 41:10

Day 12: Still Waters

In chaos loud, be still, be near,

There's peace that silences the fear.

Like water calm, so is His grace,

A quiet rest, a sacred place.

He leads you where your soul can breathe,

Beyond the noise, beyond belief.

Just trust and follow where He guides,

Still waters flow where peace abides.

"He leads me beside still waters. He restores my soul." — Psalm 23:2-3

Day 13: Speak Life

Your words hold power, don't forget,

To plant what blossoms, not regret.

Speak life to dreams, to love, to pain,

Your voice can heal, restore, sustain.

So let your mouth be streams of light,

A well of hope through the darkest night.

For when you speak from truth and grace,

You shift the winds, you shift the space.

"The tongue has the power of life and death." — Proverbs 18:21

Day 14: What You Carry

You carry joy beneath your skin,

A quiet strength, a fire within.

You've made it through what tried to end,

You broke, you healed, you learned to bend.

Don't hide your scars, they are your proof,

That faith held firm on every roof.

You carry more than pain or strife—

You carry love, light, and life.

"We have this treasure in jars of clay."

— 2 Corinthians 4:7

Day 15: Keep Sowing

The soil may seem too hard to till,

But plant the seed with patient will.

Your labor's not in vain, believe—

In time, a harvest you'll receive.

Keep sowing joy, keep sowing peace,

Your blessings planted will increase.

Though dry the ground, your hands stay true,

And God will multiply through you.

"Those who sow with tears will reap with songs of joy." — Psalm 126:5

Day 16: Divine Timing

The clock may tick, the days go fast,

But trust in God—He's never last.

Delays are not denials, Friend,

His ways are perfect in the end.

You may not see the reason yet,

But you are right where He has set.

Be still, be sure, and do not fear—

What's meant for you will soon be here.

"There is a time for everything."

— Ecclesiastes 3:1

Day 17: No Mistake

You are not broken beyond repair,

You are not lost, you're in His care.

There is no flaw He cannot use,

No shattered piece He will refuse.

You're not a burden, not too much,

You're His creation, loved as such.

So walk in grace, not guilt or ache—

You are divine, you're no mistake.

"I praise you because I am fearfully and wonderfully made."

— Psalm 139:14

Day 18: The Climb

This mountain high may test your soul,

But every step brings you your goal.

Don't rush, don't faint, don't count the cost,

For nothing climbed is ever lost.

The view from top will steal your breath,

A victory over fear, a victory over death.

So take the climb, no matter how steep,

For dreams are real to those who leap.

"The Sovereign Lord is my strength;
he makes my feet like the feet of a
deer."

— Habakkuk 3:19

Day 19: You Are Not Alone

When silence screams and no one's near,

God whispers close, "I'm always here."

You're never truly on your own,

Even in crowds, or nights unknown.

His presence wraps like a warm embrace,

A holy comfort, endless grace.

So cry, rejoice, or sit in peace—

He never leaves, His love won't cease.

"Never will I leave you; never will I forsake you." — Hebrews 13:5

Day 20: Speak to the Storm

Storms don't respond to silent cries,

But faith that speaks and testifies.

Rise up and say, "Peace, be still!"

And watch the winds obey His will.

You have the power to command,

To take your stand, with lifted hands.

So speak with boldness, speak with might—

The darkest night will yield to light.

"Even the winds and the waves obey him." — Mark 4:41

Day 21: Created for More

You weren't born to just survive,

But thrive, burn, and be alive.

Your dreams are not too big or bold,

They're whispers from His heart of gold.

So dare to live beyond the line,

You were created by design.

Shake off the dust, unlock the door—

You're destined, chosen, made for more.

"We are God's handiwork, created in Christ Jesus to do good works." — Ephesians 2:10

Day 22: Rest is Holy

You hustle hard, you chase, you strive,

But don't forget you're more than drive.

Even the sun must bow to night,

Even the stars pause in their flight.

Rest is not failure, it is wise,

A sacred gift beneath the skies.

Lay down your load, be still and know—

In quiet grace, your strength will grow.

"In repentance and rest is your salvation, in quietness and trust is your strength."

— Isaiah 30:15

Day 23: Glory in the Grind

The grind is not a sign you're low,

It's where the deepest virtues grow.

In daily tasks, and duties small,

There lies the glory of the call.

So honor what the world might miss,

The faith to show up, clean and kiss.

There's power in the unseen place—

A crown awaits the steady pace.

"Whatever you do, work at it with all your heart." — Colossians 3:23

Day 24: Nothing Wasted

The pain you felt, the nights you cried,

They shaped the wisdom deep inside.

The detours, breaks, the things delayed,

They all were part of what God made.

No tears are lost, no time is vain,

All things will bloom from the deepest pain.

So trust again, the path you tread—

There's nothing wasted when you're led.

"And we know that in all things God works for the good." — Romans 8:28

Day 25: Open Hands

Release the grip, the need to cling,

Let go and trust what God will bring.

Closed hands can't catch what's yet to fall,

But open hearts receive it all.

Let go of fear, let go of pride,

And watch what flows from Heaven's tide.

What's meant for you will surely stay—

So open wide and make the way.

"Blessed are those who trust in the Lord." — Jeremiah 17:7

Day 26: The Oil of Joy

For every tear that stained your face,

There is a joy that will replace.

God gives you oil where ashes fell,

A fragrant grace no words can tell.

You won't stay broken, won't stay down,

There is a lifting, there's a crown.

So dance again, lift up your head—

For joy will rise where sorrow bled.

"He will give you a crown of beauty instead of ashes."

— Isaiah 61:3

Day 27: The Fire Within

There is a fire you did not light,

It came from God, it burns so bright.

Though trials try to dim the flame,

It grows more fierce with every name.

You were not made to fade or flee,

You are a blaze of destiny.

So let it burn, let courage spin—

You can't go out, the fire's within.

"His word is in my heart like a fire."

— Jeremiah 20:9

Day 28: Return to Joy

Sometimes we drift, forget to sing,

Lose sight of what our joy can bring.

But joy is never far away—

It lives within, it longs to stay.

Return to laughter, light, and grace,

To dancing in your sacred space.

For joy's a gift the soul can keep—

It wakes the heart, it stirs the deep.

"The joy of the Lord is your strength."

— Nehemiah 8:10

Day 29: More Than Enough

You think you lack, you think you need,

But you are full of every seed.

The gifts, the voice, the light, the spark—

You carry all within your heart.

So stop the doubt, release the bluff—

You've always been more than enough.

Stand in your truth, don't shrink or bluff—

God made you strong, and that's enough.

"My grace is sufficient for you."

— 2 Corinthians 12:9

Day 30: The Final Word

This is the word that seals it all:

You will not break, you will not fall.

His love, your anchor—deep and wide,

His grace, your constant source and guide.

No matter what the past has said,

His promises are life instead.

He writes the end, He lifts your head—

You rise again, full Spirit-led.

"Being confident of this, that he who began a good work in you will carry it on to completion." — Philippians 1:6

Closing Prayer:

Lord, Thank You for walking with me through these 30 days of reflection, renewal, and revelation. May each word I've read become life in me, and every truth I've embraced take root deep within my spirit. Strengthen my faith, ignite my hope, and restore my joy. Let Your love continue to guide my steps and light the path ahead. As I go forward, remind me that I am never alone—for You are with me, within me, and working through me.

Amen.

About the Author:

Mike Williams is a visionary writer, musician, and faith-based storyteller committed to crafting powerful narratives that stir the soul. His work often blends spiritual depth, emotional truth, and poetic beauty to inspire transformation and reflection. This devotional is a reflection of his own journey of healing, purpose, and divine encounter. When he's not creating, Mike is mentoring artists, composing music, and helping others rediscover their voice and value through creative expression.

Made in the USA
Columbia, SC
12 June 2025

59365774R00037